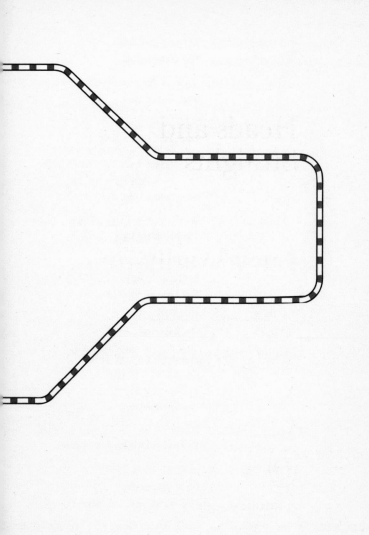

Heads and Straights

Lucy Wadham

PENGUIN BOOKS

PENGUIN BOOKS

Published by the Penguin Group
Penguin Books Ltd, 80 Strand, London WC2R ORL, England
Penguin Group (USA) Inc., 375 Hudson Street, New York, New York 10014, USA
Penguin Group (Canada), 90 Eglinton Avenue East, Suite 700, Toronto, Ontario,
Canada M4P 2Y3 (a division of Pearson Penguin Canada Inc.)
Penguin Ireland, 25 St Stephen's Green, Dublin 2, Ireland (a division of Penguin Books Ltd)
Penguin Group (Australia), 707 Collins Street, Melbourne, Victoria 3008, Australia
(a division of Pearson Australia Group Pty Ltd)
Penguin Books India Pvt Ltd, 11 Community Centre, Panchsheel Park, New Delhi – 110 017, India
Penguin Group (NZ), 67 Apollo Drive, Rosedale, Auckland 0632, New Zealand
(a division of Pearson New Zealand Ltd)
Penguin Books (South Africa) (Pty) Ltd, Block D, Rosebank Office Park, 181 Jan Smuts Avenue,
Parktown North, Gauteng 2193, South Africa

Penguin Books Ltd, Registered Offices: 80 Strand, London WC2R ORL, England

www.penguin.com

First published in Penguin Books 2013
003

Copyright © Lucy Wadham, 2013
All rights reserved

The moral right of the author has been asserted

Set in 11.75/15pt Baskerville MT Std
Typeset by Jouve (UK), Milton Keynes
Printed in England by Clays Ltd, St Ives plc

ISBN: 978-1-846-14639-8

www.greenpenguin.co.uk

Penguin Books is committed to a sustainable
future for our business, our readers and our planet.
This book is made from Forest Stewardship
Council™ certified paper.

ALWAYS LEARNING

For Mum and Dad

The first time I admitted publicly to having been brought up in Chelsea I was thirty-five and at the launch party for my first novel, which was being held in a tapas bar in Clapham. At that stage in my writing career I wasn't aware that I was allowed guests of my own, so it was just myself, the sales team from my publishing house, a handful of book reps and some booksellers. After supper we pushed back the tables and danced. It was easily the most fun I've had at a literary event. For much of the evening I talked to a woman called Luthfa, who worked for one of the book chains. She was

Bengali and had been raised in East London. She had a deep laugh and an irreverent turn of mind and I found myself wanting her to like me. She told me about the book world that I was entering, how much she had loved it and how it was doomed. We shared our experiences of the eighties and our feelings about Thatcher and her legacy, and we discussed how much life in Britain had changed in the thirteen years since I had left for France. At last she asked me where I was brought up. Usually I would stay vague about the borough of my youth or, when pressed, lie and say Putney, where I had lived briefly as a teenager, but this time I confessed. She teased me gently about being a Chelsea girl, as I knew she would, and then gave me a brief lecture about the misguidedness of trying to conceal my background. Complexes like mine, she suggested, were reductive and led to a skewed and paltry view of life.

Soon afterwards I heard that Luthfa had left the book trade and we have not met since. Strange how a single encounter can so deeply affect your view of yourself. Had it not been for that conversation I doubt I would be attempting to write about my Chelsea upbringing now. It was Luthfa who, in the wake of her own struggle to extricate herself from her background, gave me permission.

Inverted snobbery was embedded in my sisters and me from an early age, so being from Chelsea was never a source of pride for any of us. I don't know where this class shame came from, certainly not from our parents. Dad liked to pore over his family tree, claiming that his ancestors could be traced back to the Plantagenets, an assertion for which I have never found any proof whatsoever, and Mum seems undisturbed by the fact that she often sounds like the Queen. Nor did it come from our Home-Counties, pink-gin-quaffing grandparents, or even from our wild, bohemian grandmother, whose wildness, I'm sure, sprang in part from her sense of entitlement.

Not all of us went as far to dissemble our background as my elder sister, Florence (Fly), did. By the time she had turned sixteen she had changed her accent and adopted the 'Mockney' that would distinguish her from her four sisters who, in 1976, still sounded like Jenny Agutter from *The Railway Children*. By then it was easy for Fly to slip free of class boundaries. Punk rock had set up its headquarters on the King's Road, three minutes' walk from our house, and armed with her new voice and all the right gear she enrolled as a full-time rebel, no questions asked. At night, after our parents had gone to bed, she would steal my dad's BMW 320 and cruise up and down the King's Road in it, Mohawks protruding from the open roof. Today, when I ask her, she says she has no doubt that there were other posh girls in hiding with the gangs that haunted the Water Rat, the Roebuck and the Cadogan, but at that time, where you came from didn't matter half so much as whether or not you had balls.

Armed with the battle scars of the punk movement and a long fight with addiction, Fly eventually escaped to Australia and returned home years later to settle in Peckham. I, along with my two other big sisters, Izzy and Beatrice, ran away to France, where, as foreigners, we could elude the delineations of class. Indeed the only prejudice we encountered on arriving in Paris in the mid eighties was the presumption that all English girls were easy lays, a presumption that, in our case, happened to be true.

My sister Izzy, who recently attended an alumnae reunion of St Paul's Girls' School, said that there was something suffocating about being in a roomful of people who seemed to look and speak and think alike. Perhaps ours was simply the fear of seeing our individuality watered down – just another of the multifarious manifestations of snobbery, the means by which we lord it over other people.

I don't often go to Sloane Square, the Tube station nearest to where I grew up. I would not go to Peter Jones again, the scene of so much childhood boredom and frustration: waiting for what felt like hours in the shoe department

after school, amusing myself by building up
static with my socks on the thick, green carpet
and then trying to shock my mother with my
fingertips.

On the few occasions when I've been back
and walked along the King's Road, it has felt
to me like a place divested of all idiosyncrasy.
Instead of the old thoroughfare of tribal display
and rebellion, the *passeggiata* of punkdom, I
find nothing but a strip of upmarket retail and
desirable real estate. Today it is hard to imagine
how this could have been the teeming Petri
dish of counter-cultural innovation that it once
was. I look at the yummy mummies in their
cashmere and remind myself that they were
here too at that time (my own mother being
one), nipping out from behind their railings
to run the gauntlet, past the punks outside
the Chelsea Drugstore, past the patchouli-
and pot-scented emporium of shadiness that
was the Great Gear Trading Company, to
scurry into one of their safe zones: the Royal
Hospital Gardens or Peter Jones. Nowadays,

however, these men and women with ski tans and highlights no longer have to contend with a population hostile to them permanently occupying the street. I take another look at the perfectly groomed young woman pushing a pram that looks like it was designed by NASA and feel a stab of sympathy for my mother, who tried so hard to bring her girls up in her own image, but who could not possibly contend with the terrifying force the King's Road had become at that precise moment in history. One minute her daughters were dressed in tweed coats with velvet collars, lace tights and Start-Rite patent-leather shoes; the next they were bemoaning US imperialism, advocating free love and walking the strip between World's End and Sloane Square with bare feet and no knickers.

Like most acts of rebellion, our repudiation of SW3 began with refusal; in the case of my three elder sisters, the refusal to emulate the lives of their parents. Back then my father referred to himself as an entrepreneur. The younger son of divorced parents, he had been told by his father that there was not enough money to send him to Oxford. His elder brother went to Wadham College (founded by a pious and wealthy ancestor called Dorothy), an injustice, as my father saw it, from which he never quite recovered. My mother, who is mistress of the unspoken, always led us to believe that Dad was the handsome, charming one, and his elder brother the bright one, by which she meant that he probably wouldn't have got in anyway. Back in 1974 he did not care as much as he later would, because he was rich. His successful PR business was paying for three houses: the one in Chelsea, another in Berkshire and one in the South of France, two cars and the private education of his increasingly wayward daughters. For Mum and Dad the taboos about displaying your wealth that were dear to their own parents' generation had disappeared during the fifties of their youth. Like the generations that would follow them, they cared about

interior decor and food. All through the
seventies, as we grew up, our house seemed
to be in a state of constant redecoration, with
rooms being tented or stippled or dragged,
mostly with variations of the colour coral.
Mum and Dad were proto-foodies, who served
elaborate, continental recipes from Robert
Carrier at their dinner parties and sent their
offspring to school smelling of garlic, something
for which they received a written rebuke from
my headmistress.

To the Big Three, as my parents called my
three elder sisters, this ease and plenty was
stultifying. Although at the time they saw their
defiance in political terms, as scorn for the
trappings of privilege and also, of course, for
the patriarchy, it may have been more a matter
of a certain failure in the redistribution process,
for my parents kept them on a short financial
leash. Izzy believes that they might have been
less angry as teenagers if they had been bought
off just a little. As it was, lack of pocket money
meant that they were all waitressing from the

age of sixteen and very soon their hard-earned tips were funding a full-blooded rebellion.

I was ten in 1974. Fly was fifteen, Izzy was seventeen and Beatrice was eighteen. The Big Three possessed at that time an unwitting loveliness combined with a keen appetite for adventure that made them a permanent source of anxiety to my parents, and to my mother in particular. Increasingly, she pictured the King's Road as an evil force field that threatened constantly to engulf her daughters. Unbeknownst to her, Izzy had already had a narrow escape while posing naked for a white-haired sleazebag called Godfrey, who sat outside the Picasso café masquerading as a fashion photographer and picked up girls with the question, 'Did you know you could be a model?' Eight years later, he approached me and used exactly the same line. I cannot remember what I said but I have never been any good at put-downs, so it would certainly have been lame. I've always wished that I had Fly's withering repartee. I once heard her respond to a wolf whistle with 'I wouldn't fuck you for practice'.

The King's Road, as my mother knew, was awash with drugs. For my sisters the world was divided between 'Heads' (good) and 'Straights' (bad). Heads were people who smoked pot and Straights were people who didn't. In time these two categories would broaden to include, on the one hand, people who are cool, spontaneous and open-minded, and, on the other, people who have a tendency to play safe. Heroin was still seen as a drug for rebellious middle-class kids in search of a rock-and-roll aura, rather than the social disease it would later become, so none of my sisters had ruled out trying it.

Izzy played Wendy that year in a musical production of *Peter Pan*, a co-production between the boys at Westminster and the girls from St Paul's. I have never been more bewitched by a performance, before or since. I sat in awe, watching my big sister flying about the stage on wires, dressed in a long, white, Laura Ashley nightie, her blonde hair flowing, my ears burning with pride. I remember the hall erupting into wild laughter when she said in her clear, high voice: 'I've never kissed a boy before!' She now tells me that she was stoned on opium during that performance and that the boy who played John beside her Wendy introduced her to LSD a few days later. She remembers running terrified with him up and down the King's Road, goblins in pursuit. The same boy, when she dumped him, set up camp across the road from our house and spent days and nights under a broken black umbrella, gazing up at her window, willing her to take him back into her bed. I thought she was mad for rejecting him and would lie in bed at night, with the nursery window open, my hair spread out on the pillow in readiness and imagine him flying up to my windowsill like Peter Pan and kissing me in my sleep.

By the end of the following year, two of the Big Three had tried heroin. Beatrice would wait until she had escaped to Paris, where she would, like Izzy, use it recreationally throughout her twenties. For Fly, whose desire to escape her background burned the strongest, the drug was a quick route to the underworld. She would become trapped down there and for many years her addiction would effectively rub out all the distinguishing marks of her class, nearly killing her in the process.

By 1976, the rows had become so bad at home, particularly with Izzy, that my parents began casting about for a solution. Beatrice was soon to leave for Bristol University to read French, but Izzy, whose thirst for freedom was now making her openly assert her right to experiment with as many drugs and sleep with as many boys as she liked, had become dangerous. She needed to be kept away from me and my eight-year-old sister, Cissy, because we both worshipped her. My parents decided that it was too late for Fly, but we, the last two, might still be redeemable. So Izzy was billeted with friends of theirs in Fulham, where she got a job working in a local Spanish restaurant.

She tried to augment her income by selling dope to kids from the French Lycée in South Kensington, but she got caught and was asked to leave St Paul's before taking her A-Levels. She moved to a squat in Willesden, enrolled in City and East London College and severed all links with her middle-class life.

I missed Izzy. Most nights she would sing me and Cissy to sleep: Joan Baez, Dylan, Cat Stevens, numbers from the musical *Hair*, including the famous and then unintelligible song 'Sodomy'.

'Masturbation,' she would sing sweetly, as she stroked my hair, 'can be fun. Join the holy orgy, Kama Sutra . . . Every*one*!'

Izzy would only come and see us when Mum and Dad were away on their annual skiing holiday and our maternal grandmother, Eileen, would come from Wales to look after us. As a bohemian intellectual, a nature lover and a child of the suffragette movement, Eileen had little respect for the world we were being brought up in. She disapproved greatly of TV, which stayed off for the duration of her stay. Under normal circumstances, Cissy and I would switch it on every day when we came home from school and watch it for two straight hours, from the mesmerizingly banal *Play School* to the mute and psychedelic *Crystal Tipps and Alistair*. With Gran, we were expected to play, paint, read or listen to her stories. She also disapproved of money and most of the things it could buy. Her scorn for my father the entrepreneur was palpable, as would be her scorn for Laurent, the French management consultant whom I would later marry. On her eightieth birthday we threw a party for her and when I suggested that my new husband sit next to her, she looked past him at me and said with a stony glare, 'I should rather like to have my own kin around me.'

Her brand of snobbery was different to that of our parents and unbeknownst to us, her tastes and prejudices would have a deep and lasting influence. She certainly nourished the recklessness in all of us, for, as we were growing up, she read to us, beautifully and compellingly, carefully chosen novels that expressed her bohemian, romantic leanings: *Lorna Doone*, *Ivanhoe*, *Wuthering Heights*. She believed in all the big abstract nouns with capitals, Love and Art and Beauty and Truth, and in following your heart and living with passion. She married three times and spent her later years with a lover twenty-nine years her junior. Izzy recently confessed a childhood fantasy that she is sure came from Gran. 'I didn't want to marry a suitable boy and settle down,' she told me. 'I'd dream of going to the altar with one and then a tousle-haired gypsy showing up to carry me off.' Fly and I didn't love David Cassidy or Donny Osmond. We loved what my father called 'rough trade': Oliver Reed from *Oliver!* and Alan Bates from *The Go Between*.

Eileen's intellectual snobbery did not come from her parents. Her father, whom she always described as a man of letters, was also an entrepreneur, but she preferred to emphasize the fact that he spoke seven languages. In 1916 he bought a weekend cottage in a little village called Rodmell on the Sussex Downs. Three years later Virginia and Leonard Woolf moved into the cottage next door. Gran was seven. Virginia was thirty-seven. Something about my grandmother must have appealed to the novelist, who was as discerning and uncompromising about children as she was about everything else in her life. Virginia allowed her, so long as she didn't talk, to accompany her on her long walks. She must have seen something in my grandmother, something 'fine' as she might have put it, and touching.

Eileen was small for her age, exceptionally bright and emotionally insecure. When she was four she had been taken by her father to Victoria Station along with her elder sister and her two elder brothers and asked to make a choice. At first she didn't understand. There on the platform, dressed in cream silk, stood her beautiful, red-haired mother, Elspeth, whom her husband had recently repudiated and banished to Wales on the grounds that she was 'a secret drinker'.

'Choose, baby!' urged her elder brother, Ernest. 'Who do you want to go with, Mama or Papa?' Her siblings had no difficulty choosing their father, with his servants and his yacht, over their disgraced and penniless mother, and they stood resolutely beside him, but little Eileen ran to her mother and buried her face in the soft pleats of her long skirt. Elspeth held her child's head for a moment, then tore herself away and ran off down the platform.

Eileen would not see her mother again until she was fifteen. In the intervening years she was hothoused by her fierce and exacting father and punished or cajoled by a string of short-lived mistresses, all of whom found her insolent and wild. Her closest friend was her collie, Duke, with whom she would sometimes sleep in the garden, under the stars.

At last, she was caught 'necking' with a boy

in the stables and her father decided it was time she went to live with her mother. One fine spring morning in 1927, Twig, the chauffeur drove Eileen and Duke to Paddington Station and waited with her under the giant clock on Platform 1. Elspeth hadn't seen her child for eleven years. They embraced awkwardly, the dog in between their feet. On the journey, they sat in silence, neither of them willing, after their painful separation, to sink to artificial conversation. Elspeth read her newspaper and Eileen stared at the tinted photographs of Western Super-Mare above her mother's head, occasionally letting her gaze stray downwards to the elegant, auburn-haired stranger opposite her. At last, a man with a moustache, wearing a bowler hat and a dark suit opened the door of their carriage and asked if he might join them. He was a welcome distraction and they both encouraged him to sit down.

'Captain Bolton,' he said, bowing slightly and removing his hat. 'Royal Horse Artillery, stationed at Newport.'

The three of them had lunch together in the dining car and when they parted on Newport Station platform, Bolton, who on the journey had offered to teach Eileen to ride, gave Elspeth his card.

Elspeth had set up home in Newport with a postman called Nick and earned her living writing the women's page of the *Western Mail*. Eileen quickly warmed to Nick, who was kind and gentle to her. She was impressed by their library and by the beautiful, scented garden her mother had made behind their little terraced house. Every evening the two of them would walk their dogs along the banks of the river Usk, slowly overlaying the lost years with endless talk. They found that they both cared about the same things: books, paintings, flowers, birds and dogs. 'I had never known such a feeling of being wanted and loved,' my grandmother later wrote to me. 'And I responded with all my heart.'

It was there in Newport that her affection for

'the simple life' must have been born, and also, perhaps, her perplexing prejudices relating to gardens. When I eventually had a garden of my own she insisted I cut down an ornamental cherry tree that was growing happily in the middle of the lawn. 'It's a common little thing,' she said. 'Get rid of it.' And to my embarrassment, I obeyed.

What a relief it was to Eileen that her mother cared about the 'finer things in life'. Here was a woman Virginia Woolf would have approved of; a working woman, with a room of her own, who painted and read and believed in Beauty and Truth. For the seeds of my grandmother's intellectual snobbery had been planted there, on those silent walks with Virginia. She told me that even as a child she had sensed the whirring of that great mind. She would have to run to keep up with the writer as she strode across the fields, hashing out the negative space of her first experimental novel, *Jacob's Room*, about loss and the baffling and devastating trauma that they had all been through with the Great War. Eileen would always remember her own terror, aged five, at seeing a fully grown man fall to the pavement on Kensington High Street, clutching his head, and her father ushering her into a cab, muttering, 'Shell shock, baby. It's shell shock, poor fellow.' As a seven-year-old, walking with Virginia, she would have been able to hear the sound of cannon coming across the Sussex Downs, like the dull thud of 'nocturnal women beating great carpets'.*

Years later, my grandmother's home in the Brecon Beacons would be filled with copies of Woolf's novels, letters and diaries. I inherited these, along with her passion for the writer, a passion that helped me, an academic outsider with a poor school record, to pass the entrance exam to Oxford. I wrote about the uses of memory in Woolf's fiction, whole tracts of which I had learnt by heart. I was staying with Gran when the acceptance letter arrived. She

* *Jacob's Room* (1922).

was ironing and didn't even look up when I cried out in disbelief.

'Of course you got in, my dear,' she said. 'They'd be mad not to take you.'

I remember her standing there smiling at me. By then she had a deeply lined face, a long, hawk-like nose and a snaggle of tobacco-stained teeth. She wore her magnificent, long, dark auburn hair, which even to her death was barely touched with grey, in two long plaits folded on top of her head. As an old lady, she favoured trainers and stiff cotton artist's smocks, which came in two colours, navy and tomato red. The three, large pockets at the front were for her baccy (Golden Virginia), her dog treats and her pruning shears; perfect, my father would say, for the easy castration of overweening males. Gran never had any time for her son-in-law, or any of the men her granddaughters would marry. Like many of the proto-feminists of her day, she did not have a high regard for men, most of whom she saw as spineless and domineering, like her father.

Eileen's love of Virginia Woolf was all-encompassing. It embraced not only the woman's work but also her prejudices: the championing of Art above Commerce and the belief in Beauty as a portal to Truth. She passed on Woolf's love of nature to us, teaching us the names of trees and flowers, an old-world knowledge that would make us ridiculous to future boyfriends. Her cure for birds that fell from their nests was a short spell in her bra. I'll never forget the sight of a revived baby blackbird flying out of her bosom.

Woolf's withering scorn for middle-class aspiration, her voice and her manner and her bizarre pronunciation, influenced Eileen to such an extent that whenever I want to hear my grandmother's voice again, I only have to go on to YouTube and listen to the one surviving recording of Virginia Woolf talking about the English language and its uses. Our grandmother's Edwardian English made us squeal with laughter. When we were with her, pronunciation seemed to be a constant trap lying in wait for us. However you thought something should be pronounced, for Gran it was the opposite. The mountain range should be pronounced 'Himarlias', with the accent on the second syllable. You were supposed to pronounce necessarily and customarily and all the 'arily' words with the stress on the first syllable and when she read to us she would roll her 'r's, say nardays for nowadays and whenevar for whenever.

Gran's Welsh cottage was freezing and you had to put fifty p in the meter for hot water, so she often read to us in bed beneath an eiderdown so thick and heavy it was like lying under another body. Her bed was large and we would often all squeeze in with her – 'Plenty of room, come along, shove up' – and fall asleep to her radio, which she would tune to the shipping forecast, one of the few voices that still mirrored her own.

So there was Gran, busy shaking the tree, while Mum and Dad were trying to keep us under control. She clearly took pleasure in the chaos brought by my sisters' rebellion against what she saw as her daughter's narrow, middle-class lifestyle. When it was my turn to begin my sex life she invited me and my seventeen year-old boyfriend to stay. We couldn't believe our luck. She let us lie in bed all day covering each other in baby oil and brought us cups of tea and breakfast in bed. When we had gone she called my mother to say: 'You do know she's no longer a virgin, don't you, darling?'

Poor Mum didn't want to give her own renegade mother the pleasure of knowing something about her child that she didn't, so she replied 'Of course I knew'.

It was always hard to discern fact from fiction with my grandmother, a trait that drove my mother mad, but that we, as children, could appreciate. She was free with the truth and the story of her rich life changed with each telling. She was also somewhat free with private property. In Wales she encouraged us to steal fruit from other people's orchards and, unlike Mum, would never put us through the shame of taking back something we had nicked. She also had a pathological dislike for traffic cones (long before disliking traffic cones would become a national trait) and we would sit in the back of the car and watch her confiscate them. When she thought they were too plentiful she would stop, pick them up and put them in the back of her Austin Minivan.

Her dislike of authority figures was born, in part, from a feeling of class superiority, for she didn't consider that the rules governing most people applied to her. She was someone I knew instinctively must be kept away from my teachers and while she was looking after us I made sure that she never came too close to the school gates. She was also a born atheist and said that Church was the place we were least likely to find God. Before my elder sisters were brought back to London, she told them that the nuns running their boarding school were almost certainly sex-starved lesbians.

It was Gran who first taught us to question authority. In the late sixties, Paul, one of her two sons, came back from San Francisco, where he had been celebrating the Summer of Love with a six-week binge on LSD. His body came back, that is, but not all of his mind. He began to experience agonizing headaches. By the early seventies he had changed his name to Jesus and could be seen walking up and down Baker Street in a long robe, carrying a heavy Bible. He was, and is, a very smart and funny individual, and the diagnosis of paranoid schizophrenia that was made back then did not sit well, either with him or with Gran, who eschewed all advice to have him committed and invited him to move in with her to the little house she was renting on the New King's Road. She was infinitely tolerant of him and his increasingly impenetrable ways, remarking only that he'd never get a job if he insisted on signing his application letters 'Jesus Ah So'.

My parents were, by this stage, afraid of Uncle J. He had started writing them letters in feverish script with no punctuation about the end of the world and reincarnation, and while Gran was visiting her other son in America, he had, with the idea of helping her to make a fresh start on her return, put all her possessions in a pile in the back garden of the house and set fire to them. It was shortly after this that she would leave London for the Brecon Beacons, taking Uncle J with her. When I asked her years later how she had felt about the fire, she gave me her son's version: it had been a useful purge. The only two things she regretted losing were the oil painting of her as a young woman in her riding habit by her artist friend, Edward Baird, and her Remington 'noiseless typewriter'.

Mum and Dad, however, decided that this was the last straw and, while she was in America and without telling her, they had Uncle J committed to an asylum where he was rolled up in a mattress and given electric shock treatment. As soon as Gran got back to England she went to see him. He was deathly pale, and thin. He had bruises on his body and tears streaming down his face. She took him home there and then and never let the psychiatric community near him again.

There was an absurd, unspoken pact between Gran and my parents concerning Uncle J. They did not want us seeing him, but as long as they didn't actually know he was there, they went on letting us go to Wales. When we came home, they didn't ask and we didn't tell. We simply talked around the bits of our holidays that had involved our 'mad uncle'.

He could sometimes be a little alarming. His habit, for instance, of squeezing your head between his hands when he had one of his HAs (headaches) to let you know what it felt like. Or his tendency when he was telling you one of his labyrinthine stories, to reel off the addresses and postcodes of all the characters involved. I liked him, though. He had a beautiful smile and he played guitar and sang, mostly the Beatles and Irish folk songs. I can see him singing 'Lord of the Dance', with all five of us skipping behind him on the little stone bridge that led to Gran's cottage:

'Dance then, wherever you may be,
I am the Lord of the Dance, said he,
And I'll lead you all, wherever you may be,
And I'll lead you all in the dance, said he.'

Gran would send us off with him for day-long walks in the Brecon Beacons. Once we passed a little hillside chapel where a wedding was in progress. Uncle J ushered us into the back row to watch. I was lost in the beauty of the ritual and the bride's dress when the vicar turned to the congregation and said, 'Therefore, if any man can show any just cause why they may not lawfully be joined together, let him speak now, or forever hold his peace.' At that moment my uncle stood and, holding up his hand, said, 'No just cause, Vicar. Carry on,' and sat down again. Izzy and Bee got the giggles, but my cheeks were on fire with the shame of it.

Once or twice while we were staying with Gran, the police came for him. One night they found him in Gran's garden, up a tree, surrounded by lit candles. I remember watching him with Cissy from our bedroom window. He hadn't, Gran assured us, done anything wrong. They just hauled him in every now and then because they were small-minded. Meanwhile, our mother was still trying to convince us that policemen were 'firm but kind'. By then we had already chosen our camp.

While I was doing my final exams, Gran came to stay with me in Oxford to help me look after my baby son, Jack. When I came home from the library one afternoon, she was sitting in the kitchen with Jack in her arms, talking to a man in a very smelly overcoat tied up with binder twine. I was not surprised. She would often walk past homeless people, observe that they needed a good, hot meal and tell them they were coming with her. She never questioned her motives for this rather Victorian behaviour, or, indeed, the effects her actions might have and I'm certain that this lack of self-doubt sprang from her belief that she was part of an enlightened ruling class with a duty to intervene wherever she saw fit.

'Lucy, this is Mike,' she said when I walked through the door.

Mike slept on the sofa for a few days, then decided that my grandmother's brand of charity coupled with hard labour was more trouble than it was worth and left after having built a set of wonky shelves.

Gran tended to put the men in her life to work. Perhaps she was making them pay for the frivolity of her own father, but as soon as a capable male stepped across her threshold, ducking to avoid the low lintel, she would chivvy him into labour: planting, wood chopping or fixing something in her ramshackle cottage. The man she shared her life with as we were growing up was a small, stocky, good-looking Macedonian called

Kole. They met in 1962 on a camping trip to Herefordshire that had been organized by a London-based youth organization that Gran worked for at the time. He was eighteen and she was forty-seven. On the last night she got a bit tipsy, took off all her clothes and dived into the River Wye. Family folklore has it that he decided in that moment, as her pale, thin body sliced into the black water, that he would never leave her.

The next morning he begged her to take him home with her, no doubt silently offering a lifetime of DIY in exchange, and she accepted. He cleaved to her from that moment until her death in April 2000 at the age of eighty-seven. They laughed together a good deal and saw the world together. When she was in her seventies they bought an old St John's ambulance which Kole converted into a rudimentary caravan, and they drove to Africa in it. They took a year, coming back through Europe and lingering in Italy, living off the pension left to her by her devoted third husband, David, who had worked for the Bank of England. On their trip Gran collected stones from the desert for Fly, whom she had started to worry about, and filled dozens of notebooks with drawings and impressions of the people and places she saw. She and Kole must have been having sex right up to the end of her life because when she was eighty she confided to my appalled mother that she still enjoyed 'a ruddy good orgasm'. A few years before she died, though, she seemed to tire of him, because she began packing him off to his parents in Skopje for half the year. He would return every spring, fix whatever was broken and chop her wood for the following winter, when she would boot him out again.

By 1975 my parents were doing their best to disguise their fifties programming and keep in step with the age. Mum, a leggy redhead with, as my dad often boasted, a Rita Hayworth smile, bought a pair of scarlet hotpants and wore them to the King's Road Sainsbury's. Dad began sporting a look that was part public school, part hipster. He wore a pungently goaty Afghan coat over his three-piece suits and with the Jensen Interceptor he was now driving, the Bay Rum he was splashing on his face in the mornings, the St Christopher medallion he was wearing round his neck, and the Havana cigar he often held between his teeth, he became part of that hybrid species that had started to flourish all over London: the gentleman spiv. Looking at photos taken of my parents at that time, they seem dazzlingly glamorous, but to my older sisters they were two embarrassing Straights masquerading as Heads.

As a couple they must have had some magnetism because the house was always full of liggers and they weren't always there for the Big Three. There was Dave from the Peabody Estate, whom Izzy brought home once and who, I see it now, took one look at my mother and fell in love. He seemed to be there every day when we came home from school, sitting in our basement kitchen, roasting himself beside the Aga, drinking tea with Mum and making her laugh. He taught her Cockney

rhyming slang and she would swiftly cite their
friendship if anyone dared to call her a snob.
My father tolerated him, calling him Porridge
(his surname sounded similar) and using him
as a kind of class snitch.

'Have you ever slept with a black woman,
Porridge?' he once asked.

'No, Giles. I haven't actually.'

'Tell me when you do, will you?'

'Certainly.'

Then there was the Dane. No one ever knew
his real name, or anything much about him
except that he was Danish and very dull. He
was tall and skinny, with whitish-blond hair, bad
skin and a barely audible voice. One of Izzy's
friends brought him round once and left him in
our kitchen for what seemed like years.

'The fucking Dane's here.'

'Tell him I'm out.'

'It's your turn.'

'Fuck off. I got stuck with him for an hour the
other day. Leave him with Mum.'

'She's said no.'

After a while, the Dane stopped asking for anyone in particular and would just fall into one of the deep, low armchairs in the basement and watch the life of the family going by until someone remembered and turfed him out.

My parents struggled to keep an open mind about the endless comings and goings. Soon they were keeping to their part of the house, relinquishing the basement and top floor to my sisters. The phone rang constantly and it was always some boy asking – in that stoned drawl, peppered with the word 'man', so unique to the seventies – to speak to one of the Big Three. Cissy and I had instructions on who to dispatch and who to favour. I remember someone called 'The Owl' ringing for Izzy for months without ever getting through to her.

Mum and Dad were the hapless gatekeepers of a house that was besieged day and night by hormonal boys. There was a kernel of them who virtually lived in the basement, forcing my mother to retreat to the sitting room upstairs: 'I'm sick and tired of being stared out of my kitchen!' And then there were those who had to vie for admission.

Always welcome was our charismatic Uncle Henry. Mum's little brother and Gran's beloved elder son was a born Head. He would come over from San Francisco, where he lived and worked as a freelance writer, and appear at our back door with his wicked grin, his long hair and sideburns; six foot four and so handsome in his leather coat, his big silver-dollar belt and Mexican rings. He'd throw open his arms for Cissy and me, call us 'buddy', kiss us all full on the lips, and then we'd all settle down to listen to his stories. Most of what he related was beyond my grasp, but I was enthralled by his exotic American vocabulary and his big, contagious laugh. He 'turned on' the Big Three to politics, telling them about the horrors of the Vietnam War and Watergate and the abuse of power in America. Izzy dates her feminism back to her meeting with Diane, one of Henry's sassy Californian girlfriends whom he brought to the basement once. She looked like Ali McGraw and, for Izzy, everything about her seemed to augur a much bolder, brighter future for women. Henry wrote for *True*, the magazine 'for today's adventurous male': exciting news stories about the Baader Meinhoff group, Black Power, Patty Hearst and the Getty kidnapping. He also wrote for *Car and Driver* magazine and often had a sports car that he was test-driving for them, and sometimes he would challenge Dad, who viewed him with a pained mixture of envy and admiration, to a race down Park Lane at night. Poor Mum would endure his visits in those days with tight-lipped forbearance. As far as she was concerned her brother, like her mother, was a loose cannon.

And she was not wrong. To the girls, Henry was the guru of Heads. Only ten years younger than Mum, Henry saw himself as the same generation as her daughters. It used to drive her mad that he would always choose to go straight down to the basement when he flew in, instead of going to greet her and Dad in the sitting room. She knew, because he never took

pains to disguise it, that he smoked pot with
her older girls and that it was he who provided
the words and music to their rebellion. He gave
Beatrice *Layla* by Derek and the Dominoes and
sat listening to Jimi Hendrix's *The Cry of Love*
with them and *American Beauty* by the Grateful
Dead. He gave Izzy Germaine Greer's *The
Female Eunuch*, and confirmed to them all that
they were right to challenge the tastes and
attitudes of their elders. On Izzy's sixteenth
birthday he sent her a return ticket to San
Francisco. Mum intercepted it and spirited
it away.

The seventies marched on and the colours
on the King's Road turned slowly from rainbow
to black. In 1976 a fracture opened up between
my three eldest sisters. Izzy and Beatrice still
favoured cowboy boots with long, embroidered,
Arthurian dresses that came from a shop on
the Kings Road called Forbidden Fruit, but Fly
moved to black drainpipes and brothel creepers.
Gradually the punks edged out the hippies
and places like Gandalf's Garden gave way to

places like Vivienne Westwood's shop, SEX.
Just walking, aged twelve, past that place, the
rudest word in the world towering over me in
huge, wet-look pink letters, made my heart race.
Everything about the world Fly was entering
terrified me: the look, the language, the attitude.
She painted her room black and forbade me to
enter. Sometimes, when she was out, I would
sneak in to look at her things: her panoply of
silk scarves, her silver bangles that covered
her wrists like armour, her dressing table with
her kohl, her black nail varnish, her peacock
feathers. Her clothes were an amalgam of
Beardsley, carnival and punk rock. Every time
she went out at night, she was pushing some
kind of look. She had a black cowboy suit with
white piping and when she wore it with her
cowboy boots, she strode like a man. She started
telling me to fuck off if I dared speak to her
at the breakfast table, and swiping me round
the head with her bangled arm when I pissed
her off, which was most of the time. Beatrice
and Izzy, the only family members she could

tolerate, had left London by then, Beatrice for Bristol and Izzy to live on a commune near Oxford.

When she wasn't being grounded, Fly was out on the King's Road, usually upstairs at the Cadogan, where the barman turned a blind eye to underage drinking. She never brought anyone home except on the rare occasions when she had the house to herself. One Sunday night my parents came back from the country, Cissy and me in tow, and walked into their bedroom to find her and a young man with a freckled face and green-and-ginger-spiked hair leaping from their preposterous four-poster bed. Spike, as he was then known, advanced, naked, towards my appalled father, hand outstretched. I don't remember this, but I do remember the unsettling sight of Spike tugging his tartan bondage trousers on over his lily-white bottom as he shambled off down the corridor. Years later, when Fly and I were at a party, he was introduced to me as a landscape gardener called Steven Pike. I became his girlfriend and soon discovered where we'd met before.

Sleeping with each other's boyfriends was seen as an inevitable hazard of our closeness as sisters and perfectly acceptable provided a decent time lapse was observed. Laurent, my French husband, had been Beatrice's boyfriend before he was mine. The value of sharing is so deeply ingrained in us as to seem, to many, dizzyingly boundaryless: shared boyfriends, towels, toothbrushes, even university degrees. Izzy would later borrow Beatrice's degree to get her first job in publishing.

Mum became more and more appalled by the spectacle of her daughters' adolescence. She read Margaret Mead's *Coming of Age in Samoa* in an attempt to make sense of it all, but it didn't help. She would impose absurd curfews and then sit on the stairs, fretting, in her nightdress, hours after they had been missed. Phobic as she was about conflict, she would try in vain to get my father to apply the principle of consequence to their behaviour. The chaos of their emancipation reminded her of her own wild mother and filled her with a sense of dread, particularly when we all began to show such a deep devotion to Eileen. After all Gran was a Head and Mum would forever be a Straight.

Back then we were all too dazzled by Gran's strength and charisma to see how hard it must have been for Mum to have been her child. The two of them could hardly have been more different and when Mum talks about Eileen, even when she is speaking with fondness, she still manages to convey the sense of a deep, unspoken injury too painful to acknowledge. Mum was what Gran used to call her love child, as if this should pardon every blunder.

When Eileen was seventeen, Captain Bolton, the man they had met on the train, invited her and her mother to a dance at the officers' mess. Elspeth was still slim and youthful, and she and Eileen were often mistaken for sisters. As they got ready, Nick sat by the fire, listening benevolently to their excited chatter. Eileen wore a knee-length, apple-green silk dress and Elspeth a long gown made of bronze taffeta.

In the two years since her arrival in Wales Eileen had, under Bolton's tutelage, become a talented and fearless rider. Physical courage seemed to bring with it a boldness that was making her father increasingly uncomfortable. Reports from his eldest son, Ernest, reached him in London and confirmed that his youngest daughter was dreaming of becoming a vet and had already received three proposals from three different suitors. When she walked into the ballroom on that May evening in 1929 she was quite a beauty. As her elder sister, Kitty, once told Mum, 'Eileen could have had any man in England', but Eileen was not particularly interested. She wanted adventure and she sensed that marriage was the least favourable route.

At the dance she met one of Bolton's brother officers, a thirty-year-old captain called Tom Taylor. He was tall and fair and good-looking, but above all he was a crack rider, better even than Bolton. To her delight he offered to coach her in the manège. He taught her to jump, and, while doing so, to pull her loosened jumping saddle from beneath her and, while her horse was in mid-leap, brandish it above her head. She learnt fast and he watched in admiration, falling more and more deeply in love.

I don't know the details of their courtship, only that her father, increasingly concerned by her flightiness, eventually struck a bargain with her. Marry Captain Taylor, he told her, and I will buy you both a riding school of your own in Hyde Park Mews. Seeing the opportunity for a life on her own terms, she agreed. She drew out her engagement for as long as she could. She became the belle of Rotten Row, could be seen driving a four-in-hand alone across London, broke in polo ponies for the Prince of Wales and sent her fiancé mad with jealousy.

At last, shortly after her eighteenth birthday, they married. The ceremony and reception was bad enough; a grand affair, my grandmother told me, which bored her to tears, but the wedding night was much worse. Taylor lunged at her as soon as they were alone and his fervid performance after the long months of restraint convinced her never to let him near her again. A modern-day Irene Forsyte, she started keeping a gun under her pillow.

After months of pleading, cajoling and raging, Tom complained to her father. Unwilling to confront his fiery-tempered daughter on the matter of her sex life, her father summoned the vicar, who bumbled his way through a monologue on marital duty while my grandmother, dressed in her jodhpurs and impatient to leave, glared at him with unabashed contempt. When he had finished, she told him that she wanted an annulment.

A meeting was convened with Mr Life, the family lawyer. My grandmother announced her idea. Mr Life said there were absolutely no grounds for an annulment.

'Divorce, then. I want a divorce.'

'You won't get a divorce. You would have to

prove desertion, insanity, adultery or cruelty. Is your husband guilty of any of these?'

'Adultery,' my grandmother mused. 'On whose part?'

'On either part.'

Eileen smiled triumphantly. 'Then here I go to commit adultery!'

By the time she had reached the mews, she had made her choice. He was one of her pupils, a handsome, red-haired Canadian of her own age called Brian Jackson. He was a foreigner and just passing through, so he would, she believed, make no claims on her.

After their next riding lesson, she put her problem to him. She needed someone to be unfaithful with. Unsurprisingly, he agreed to help her. She made the arrangements; all he had to do was to turn up. So that was how my mother was conceived, in room number 24 of the Bridge Hotel in Epsom. The next morning Eileen and Brian ordered breakfast in bed so that the chambermaid who brought it up might later testify to their affair in court.

When she came home that evening, her portrait – the one that her son would later burn – had been turned to the wall, and Tom, poised for her return, was lying on the kitchen floor with his head in the oven. When he heard her key in the lock, he turned on the gas. Eileen walked into the kitchen, stepped over him and put another coin in the meter.

'I forgive you everything,' Tom pleaded, leaping to his feet and grabbing her.

'I don't want forgiveness,' she answered, shaking him off. 'I want divorce.'

This was my grandmother's version of the story. She says that the marriage ended there and then, and that she, discovering she was pregnant, set up on her own. But here my grandmother's narrative becomes unreliable. My mother has early memories of sitting on Tom Taylor's knee and his name is on her birth certificate, so they must have still been together when she was born.

My mother gives me a sly look and shakes her head. 'Your grandmother made it up as she went along, darling. She was a complete mythomaniac.'

What is certain is that, for Eileen, her beautiful, red-haired daughter was hers and no one else's. She called her Elizabeth, after the Virgin Queen.

Elizabeth never knew her father. Although Brian asked many times, Eileen refused to let him have any contact with his child. The price of Gran's freedom was to plant a void in my mother's psyche that would lead to an endless craving for male approval. When she was dying, Gran eventually asked for her forgiveness. My mother gave it, of course, but the remorse came far too late to be of any use to her.

With this background, it must have been hard for Elizabeth to be a mother to five girls. When I was ten and she was forty-one, she and Dad adopted a son. My sisters and I have all noted, with no feeling of resentment towards our adored brother, Joe, how much more effortlessly she loved him. His being a boy simply made it easier for her.

In the sixties Dad tried to find Mum's
father, beginning with a society photographer
called Houston Rogers, who had taken Brian
Jackson's picture in the thirties. He tracked
Jackson to Ontario, where the trail went cold.
Gran said he was a member of Bert Ambrose's
dance band, which was very popular in thirties
London. She said that he played the drums,
but I've looked at a film on YouTube of the
band playing in the Embassy Club in 1931, the
year Jackson and Eileen met. The drummer
in the film is a stout, middle-aged man. There
is, however, a young man with slicked-back
hair and a shy, dimpled smile, who is playing
the xylophone, and I wonder if this might be
my grandfather. Knowing Gran, in the telling
of her story she would have had no difficulty
upgrading the father of her child from a player
of the xylophone to the drums, a much sexier
instrument. A specialized website informs me
that 'not all Ambrose's band members have
been identified yet'. My mother had dimples;
perhaps it was the xylophone player.

By 1977 the King's Road had become the setting for a rather stagey war between punks and Teds. Like the street fights between mods and rockers in the late sixties, there was often a call to battle on Saturday nights. That year Fly left home and moved in to a flat on a brand new, red-brick housing estate in World's End. With the Big Three gone, for the first time, Cissy and I became inseparable. Rivalry for our glamorous sisters' affections quickly became solidarity against the new regime that prevailed at home. Giggling became our principal occupation as an antidote to the ambient boredom. The phone had stopped ringing, the record player had gone silent and the heady scent of pot masked by joss sticks soon faded away. Our parents reconquered the basement and within a month the atmosphere in the house had gone from exotic, high-class brothel to Trusthouse Forte.

Fly, who had by now completely changed her accent, settled into one of the seven massive tower blocks, which, as far as our parents were concerned, teemed with low life and marred the Chelsea skyline. I don't think they ever set foot into the piss-infused warren of alleys that led to Fly's building. The sentimentally named Whistler's Walk (after the Chelsea-based American painter) was strictly out of bounds to Cissy and me, but we would sometimes sneak along the King's Road to World's End to visit Fly in her new life. This revolved around a large, joint-rolling coffee table, which drew, by turns, the stalwarts of the punk movement, the newly emerging rockabillies, the two-tone skinheads and the rude boys. Cissy and I would sit amongst them, all agog, our hands folded in our laps, trying to make polite conversation in between bursts of stifled laughter, until Fly would turf us out.

Fly, along with many of the people who drifted through 'Whistlers', was a Chelsea supporter and was often at Stamford Bridge on Saturday afternoons. She fancied Chelsea captain Butch Wilkins and knew all the chants. She taught Cissy and me 'Blue is the Colour'

and regaled us with stories of after-match
violence on the streets of World's End. She
once took me to a Chelsea–Tottenham match.
All the way through, the Chelsea fans in the
sheds were shouting out a word I couldn't
understand. As we were leaving the stadium
I asked Fly what it was. 'They're shouting
"yiddo". It means Jew. I know, it's fucked.
Hurry!' She grabbed my wrist and pulled me
towards the exit. People were starting to leave
the stadium to avoid the aggro. We were pushed
down in the stands on our way out and I still
have the scar on my chin. I remember people
grabbing milk bottles from doorsteps and
smashing them to make weapons, and holding
Fly's hand as we ran down the street, mounted
policemen in pursuit.

Fly thrived on adrenalin and would never
knowingly pay on the Tube or, if she could
help it, for a gig. The following year one of
her closest girlfriends started going out with a
member of The Clash. The band was often
round at the flat in World's End and when they

became successful the new rockabilly band, The Stray Cats, replaced them. I remember meeting one of them on the sofa, introducing myself politely and after a pause asking his name. Baffled by the question he answered, as if I ought to have known, 'Slim Jim.'

'Sorry?'

'Slim Jim Phantom.'

Nervously I looked up at Fly, who was standing in the doorway giving me the Look of Death.

I persisted.

'Is Slim your first name? Or Jim? Which is your surname?'

Now it was his turn to look nervous. Who was this teenager and what did she want from him, clearly not to suck his penis for a backstage pass. He looked at Fly, then back at me waiting politely for an answer.

Poor Fly, whenever Cissy and I showed up all her careful attempts to hide her background were suddenly doomed.

By then, Fly had a serious heroin habit.

Uncle Henry was the first grown-up to spot it. He had warned her off the drug in the past and realizing that she was now an addict, decided to tell Mum, who was still fretting about the dangers of pot. In those days the colour supplements were full of articles with titles like 'How To Tell If Your Child Is Smoking Marijuana'. Neither she nor Dad had any idea how to face heroin addiction.

Fly, meanwhile, had only one concern: how to pay for her gear. Mum had found out that she had been forging her cheques and swiftly cut off that source. Then Dad's rich and elegant stepmother, Betty – whom I knew from photos as a Wallace Simpson lookalike leaning on a croquet mallet or a shooting stick – died and left each of us a dizzying five thousand pounds. Within the year Fly had spent all of hers. Freshly coached in the emergent concept of 'tough love', Mum and Dad cut off all financial help. Izzy leant on her new boyfriend, who was an assistant director, to get Fly work in the film industry. Her first job was a gift: she was to be a 'runner' on a film about a British borstal called *Scum*, starring the young Ray Winstone, who was, in those days, the paragon of working-class glamour. Fly was in her element: all those naughty boys (many of them, like Phil Daniels, recruited from Anna Scher's theatre school in Islington), trying to make the posh girl blush.

After *Scum* she got a job as third assistant director on an advert shot for Lee Cooper by the then unknown Tony Scott. The brief was to make an edgy, punk film to the soundtrack of Gary Numan singing 'Don't Be a Dummy'. On the first day of the shoot the casting agency sent over a handful of squeaky-clean actors dressed up as punks. Fly was appalled. Taking a deep breath, she stopped Tony Scott on his way out of the audition room and offered to get him the real thing. He agreed, so Fly went down to the King's Road, and with the promise of fifty quid each recruited a handful of volunteers from her old gang. The following morning she rounded them all up, squeezed them into a cab and delivered them to the set.

With her walkie-talkie radio, her chutzpah and her eloquent obscenities, Fly became a valuable element to have on a shoot. Tony Scott gave her a job at the production company he shared with his brother, Ridley, who was in the process of making *Alien*. Fly, who back then had the junkie's perspective on private property, at the end of the shoot somehow managed to nick the khaki boiler suit that Sigourney Weaver had worn in the film. It was an old NASA suit made of thick, silky material and covered in zips that laced tightly at the back and made it fit like a corset. I inherited the suit when Fly was done with it and wore it all through the eighties. It was the outfit I changed into when I took off my wedding dress.

When I was fifteen Fly left World's End and moved into a basement flat off Notting Hill Gate, which she rented with her roadie boyfriend. By then I knew that she was taking heroin. On a long car journey my mother had broken down and confided in me. They sent Fly to the Priory, a gloomy, neo-Gothic rehab clinic surrounded by dusty laurel bushes. The consultant psychiatrist asked her to make a list of every drug she had taken thus far (on the strength of which he would later tell Mum that there was no hope for her), then he very slowly and methodically took apart his Schaeffer pen and asked her if the process reminded her of fixing. Fly thought he was a twat, went through the motions in group therapy and crossed off the days until she could leave. Sleeping in the bed next to her was a woman receiving electric shock treatment for depression who moaned through the night. Fly turned twenty while she was in there and I went to visit her on her birthday. With my pocket money I'd bought her a pair of feather earrings that I'd found in the Great Gear Trading Company. I remember her opening the little box and bursting into tears. It was more of a shock to see my invincible big sister crying than it had been to find out that she was on drugs.

Fly tried several times to quit and when she did the one person she could withdraw with was Gran. She would drive down to Wales and hide out with her in her little cottage beside its roaring stream. Sometimes she would let Gran nurse her through cold turkey, but mostly she would go for a night and then race back to London to score. Gran adored Fly, recognizing in her her own vulnerability and bravado. She tried to help her fight her addiction, without ever judging her for it. On those rare occasions when Fly did manage to sit out the agony of withdrawal, Gran would take her into her bed and tell her stories from her own flawed life. Perhaps she wished to warn Fly against the same uncompromising spirit that had so often defeated her, but like the rest of us, Fly admired her all the more for her adventuring.

Gran had a theory that there were three basic types of compatibility: intellectual, emotional and sexual. A lasting relationship required two out of three of these, and one of them, she believed, had to be sex. Her second marriage, she said, was built entirely on sexual attraction and as a result, could not last.

After the audacious start to her adulthood, Gran carried on in defiance of convention, following her heart, loving and hating with equal passion and inciting equal proportions of love and hate. 'Don't let her into your life,' her second husband, Peter, once warned my father. 'She'll wreck it for you.'

When Eileen and Peter met they were both twenty-two. Eileen was living happily with her two year-old daughter, Elizabeth, running the riding school and enjoying her independence. It was love at first sight, she said; a bolt of lightning. Peter was tall and dark, his good looks offset by a beguiling shyness. He was teaching history at a boys' prep school, dreaming of making his fortune in the colonies and serving the Crown as his own father had done. To Peter, Eileen was the most glamorous creature he had ever set eyes on and he saw in her all the courage and drive he needed. Without a moment's hesitation Eileen gave up her riding school to marry him and have his children. She now wanted only one thing: to make Peter happy, so, with her usual gusto, she swung into action and, with her father's help, bought them a house in the country, found him a job in London (organizing trade shows and exhibitions with her father) and bore him three children.

Five years later, she was living happily in a large house on the Sussex Downs of her childhood, freelancing for the *Daily Express* women's page and home-schooling the children. Peter, who was commuting to London to a job that bored him, had come to feel like a stranger in his own life and an adjunct to hers. This was not the life of purpose and adventure he had dreamt of. Unwilling to confront her directly, he began to stay away for longer and longer periods, sleeping in London at his club (the Oriental), and eventually in other women's beds. Gran's version is that he was too chronically insecure to allow her to love him properly, but for my mother, Elizabeth, Eileen

suffocated Peter and thrived on the drama of
their constant rifts and reunions. Mum says that
her own fear of conflict comes from listening
to their terrifying rows. The war, when it
came, was a boon to Peter and he volunteered
immediately. Mum still remembers the pallor of
his face when he came home from Dunkirk, and
the smell of his wet uniform.

After the war Peter seems to have tried
to escape Eileen by accepting a posting in
Kenya. Six months later, determined to 'save
the marriage', she followed him, with the
four children, to a hill station 9,000 feet up
in the cedar and bamboo forests of the Mau
Escarpment. Elizabeth was fourteen, her
little sister, Mary, was nine, Henry was four
and Uncle J (then called Paul), was two. In
Nakuru, the nearest town, Eileen waited for
Peter to appear. When he did, the rows began
again for she quickly gleaned a sense of what
he had been up to for the past six months.
She described the atmosphere of ennui and
promiscuity that reigned in Nakuru at the

time as 'Happy Valley in its death throes'.
One after the other, she was introduced to the
bored, white colonial housewives who had been
entertaining her handsome husband during
his furloughs. They greeted this haughty new
bluestocking, clearly intent on spoiling the fun,
with undisguised hostility.

At last she and Peter packed and left for
his new posting. He would be 'DO' (District
Officer) of Olenguruone and it would be a new
start for their marriage. He had orders to settle
a land dispute in the Rift Valley between the
Maasai, nomadic warrior herdsmen, and the
sedentary Kikuyu farmers. Travelling with them
cross-country by jeep were an African radio
operator and five informants from the warring
tribes. Eileen had no misgivings. The boys
would love 'Olo', Peter told her. They could run
wild there, and the girls too.

The house was thirty-two miles from
Molo, the nearest town, and at the end of
an 18-mile-long dirt road. A large bungalow
with a wide veranda and a tile roof, it was set

in a lovely garden with a 'banda', a round hut with whitewashed mud walls and a 'makouti' (thatched) roof for guests. Five black servants stood on the veranda to greet Eileen. They bowed and called her 'memsahib', and she shook their hands, smiling awkwardly. According to Mum, she was never relaxed with the servants: 'How could I be,' she would ask, 'when I could feel they hated us?' Eileen shook hands with Wingula, the head boy – who, as she discreetly observed to Peter, was a man, not a boy – and with Otupa, who would be her cook, with Awanda, the chief 'houseboy', with the 'dhobi' who would do her laundry and with the 'scyce' who would look after the two horses that Peter had borrowed for her from the nearby estate.

Then two white men appeared to whisk Peter away. They were a surveyor and the local policeman, who was working with him. Eileen watched her husband climb into their jeep without a backward glance. Knowing that she had made a mistake, she rolled up her sleeves and, with a strong sense of the absurd, set about unpacking her twenty-two crates of fine furniture, pictures, records and first-edition books.

Whilst her children were exploring the outlying hills, Awanda, the head houseboy, who was not Kikuyu, but Luo (like Barack Obama's father), would try discreetly to warn her of the situation into which she had brought them. In the forests all around them, Kikuyu independence fighters were gathering under the command of a man called Lucas Kipkoech, a disciple of the charismatic leader, Elijah Masinde, leader of the Dini ya Musambwa movement. Masinde preached that the white man was the devil and that the fate of the African would never improve until he had dipped his spear in the white man's blood. This was the start of what would become the Mau Mau Uprising that would leave more than 12,000 dead and begin the end of British rule.

Gradually Eileen came to understand that Peter had brought her to a front line.

Caught between the demands of Whitehall and the Kikuyu elders, Peter felt increasingly out of his depth. Often away 'in the field', he left Eileen with a loaded shotgun, which she took to bed with her. One night a man tried to climb into her bedroom window. Fortunately she did not obey Peter's instructions, which had been to shoot first and question later, for the man had come to ask for her help. A woman in the Kikuyu village was having a difficult labour. Eileen put on her dressing gown, found a torch and followed the man through the forest to the hut where the woman was lying in agony. I don't know what my grandmother did. She had no medical training of any kind or any particular expertise but the woman apparently calmed down at the sight of this authoritative white woman in her home and delivered her baby without further incident.

Mum said that Eileen never fell in love with Kenya like she herself did, but she made the best of it. Every morning she would school the children around the dining-room table. She read the little boys *The Black Arrow*, Robert Louis Stevenson's tale of outlaws and derring-do in the forest, hoping, perhaps, that fiction would somehow override reality in their imaginations. Uncle Henry said that they felt no fear as children, only excitement at all the adventure. He remembers the sound of the Kikuyu drums at night and the thrill at the sight of the forest on fire as the Kikuyu tried to burn them out. Mum remembers evacuating the horses as the bamboo popped all around her, covering their heads with damp towels to lead them away from the inferno.

For Peter, the fire was the last straw. He handed in his notice, arguing that his family was no longer safe. He told Eileen that they would go to South Africa, where there were opportunities for him. While he was away preparing their journey, Eileen received a telegram from him instructing her to sell everything. She and Awanda organized a lawn sale. 'It was the books,' she would tell me, still smarting all those years later. 'They were the hardest things to lose.'

Then, as she was waiting with the children at the train station in Nakuru, someone handed her a telegram: 'Returning Saturday. Hold everything. Peter.'

He returned as promised, set them up in a tin-roofed bungalow beside a diatomite mine in a place called Gilgil and then disappeared in pursuit of some new opportunity upcountry. In Gilgil my mother, who was now seventeen, became engaged to Richard Campbell, the white policeman who had been working with Peter. He was, of course, tall, dark and handsome, but he was also, at the tender age of twenty-four, a war hero, having fought as a fleet air-arm pilot on the Russian convoys. A week before Mum's eighteenth birthday he was killed by a Kikuyu spear while trying to arrest Lucas Kipkoech on the shores of Lake Baringo.

Mum went to bed for several weeks. Gran,

who could never quite believe in her precious
daughter's love for any man, tried to hurry her
recovery. Only Peter seemed to understand the
depth of her grief. In those last weeks in Africa,
Mum would wake every morning to find her
stepfather sitting in a chair beside her bed.

After Richard's death at Baringo, Peter seems
to have run out of ideas. His colonial dreams
were unravelling as fast as the Empire itself.
With no clear ambition, he returned to Nairobi
to await another posting. Eileen was unwilling
to follow him into the vapid ex-pat life of the
Mathaiga Club and the Rift Valley Club and
the Norfolk Hotel, where Happy Valley types
were still trying to squeeze the last breath from
their idyll. Instead she took the children along
the coastal trail from Mombasa to the port of
Tanga and caught the ship home.

I loved listening to Mum talking about Kenya.
The stories always gripped me, as if I knew,
even as a child, that this was where she had
been her most alive. I grew up knowing
that Richard Campbell was my mother's One

True Love and always had the sense that my father would do, but didn't quite match up.

As the seventies came to a close our comfortable life in Chelsea began to fall apart. Dad's press-cuttings business, which he had milked recklessly all through the seventies to pay for our extravagant lifestyle, was failing. *The Times*, one of his main clients, went on strike for a year and this was followed by the Winter of Discontent, all of it carrying the Conservatives into power on a tide of uncollected rubbish. During this period, my flamboyant father, instead of downsizing, moved his business into smart new offices in the prophetically named Terminal House in Victoria. He also hired an expensive secretary called Frances, whom he interviewed in our sitting room at home. While pacing up and down in front of the fireplace, he spied something dark in the thick, white mohair carpet. He bent down and picked it up and it was only as he was popping it on the mantelpiece that he realized it was one of my little brother's turds. He sealed the deal with Frances by shaking her hand. Very soon she was out of a job. Thatcher's chancellor, Geoffrey Howe, had raised interest rates and Dad's firm, like so many other small businesses, went to the wall.

For Dad, 1980, the year he liquidated his company, would become the Year of the Crash. Henceforth, for him, there would be 'BC' and 'AC': before and after the crash. He tried hard to eschew bitterness. Under the influence of his Swiss skiing instructor, Otti – who fancied himself as a bit of a guru and saw the lost English public schoolboy that was my father as a prime target for reform – Dad started reading the work of the contemporary philosopher, Erich Fromm. His latest book* invited the reader to stop trying to 'have' and start trying to 'be'. That summer, I remember sitting beside Dad on a rock looking out over the Adriatic (we were on holiday in Communist Yugoslavia), listening to

* *To Have or to Be* (1976).

him talking about Fromm's teachings. It was to be our last summer together before he and Mum decided to emigrate to Australia, and I was simultaneously falling in love with a young Serbian and the idea of socialism. (Tito had just died and my holiday dreamboat, in between sustained snogging, had been recounting tales of the Communist leader's heroism and vision.) As I sat on that rock, listening to Dad's new, humanistic world view which coincided so beautifully with my own, I felt a powerful bond with this father from whom I was in the process of breaking away.

These new ideas would never properly mesh with Dad's nature and conditioning. He was a materialist to his last breath. He lived for good food, good wine and what Fly calls 'zhuzh', meaning anything posh or fancy: smart hotels and fancy restaurants, skiing, quality tailoring. Indeed, part of Dad's relief at the news that I was going to marry Laurent came from the idea that I would be living in the style to which he was accustomed. For many years my generous

French husband would pepper my father's life with expensive skiing holidays and luxury villas. It is a great credit to Dad that he hid his despair when, submitting to Gran's deep influence, I left Laurent and moved to a ruin in the Cevennes, a part of France that boasts not a single Michelin star.

On that rock Dad and I talked about our new lives, about his in Australia and mine in London. In September I would be enrolling for the first time in full-time, state education, studying for A-Levels at a sixth-form college in King's Cross. Dad would be taking Mum, Cissy and my brother, Joe, to Sydney, where no one would care which school he had attended, or whether or not he had been to Oxford. He had sold his three houses and his cars and he was ready to 'start again', but this time in a classless society and with a new set of values. I believed him, having no idea back then that he had ferreted away as much of his fortune as he was able to hide from the taxman in Switzerland which he would eke out over the next thirty years to pay for such indispensable extravagances as his annual skiing trip.

It is amazing to me to think that when Dad moved to Australia he was only forty-seven. He never tried to set himself up in business again, masking, with his newfound philosophy, a shattering loss of confidence. Instead he worked as a freelance PR consultant, adding to his income by importing and selling Guernsey sweaters door to door. His relationship with my mother, which had thrived on his glamorous view of them both, began to wither in their new, constrained circumstances. Despite his protestations to the contrary, he could never completely sever the class ties that still bound him to England. He ostentatiously transferred his loyalty to the Australian cricket and rugby teams, but speculated endlessly about how much his house in Chelsea would cost now, drooled over English stately homes, and fantasized about the life he might have had if he had done what his public-school cronies had advised and 'got straight back in there'.

It was as if he was plagued by the idea that, deep down, he was accountable as a man only in the mother country and by his own class, and that all attempts to escape that reality were somehow doomed.

Mum, on the other hand, was busy embracing her new life in a society that couldn't care less about her illegitimacy and lack of formal education. People judged her by what they found: a beautiful, amusing woman eager to start again. As Dad's inner resistance to his new life grew, he and Mum began to drift apart. Increasingly despondent and in the absence of any desires of his own, he did what she asked and left Sydney for the outback. They bought the house she had fallen in love with. Set in the verdant Southern Highlands of New South Wales, it reminded her of Kenya. Like her mother, she would breed horses, learn to drive a four-in-hand and throw herself into rural life. And like the Rift Valley where Eileen's marriage to Peter had come to an end, this idyllic place would be where she and Dad would bury their love. It was here that Mum, in the time-honoured tradition of the women in my family, fell for a man twenty-two years younger than her. Mellors, as my father would rudely refer to him (after Lady Chatterley's lover), came to build Mum some stables and within a year she had moved in with him.

Fly and I both experienced Dad's bankruptcy as a form of deliverance: Fly from expensive rehabilitation clinics and I from private school. My first day at Kingsway-Princeton College of Further Education in King's Cross was to be the first day of my new life. I was fifteen and a fully blown, self-loathing Straight. I had never slept with a boy, or taken drugs, or been to a rock concert. I thought long and hard about what to wear on that first day in September 1980 and when I walked into the cafeteria I realized that I had made a mistake. I had chosen a hand-me-down outfit from Fly's wardrobe: a V-shaped, brown and white mohair skirt with Peruvian motif and matching jumper (the sort recently repopularized by Detective Inspector Sara

Lund of *The Killing*), with suede moccasin boots.
Suddenly I realized that I looked like a roaring
Sloane. As I filled my tray, found a table and
sat down, I felt as if I had 'Made in Chelsea'
stamped all over me. Hoping to disappear, I
talked to no one that day and vowed to blend
in better in future. After that I stuck to jeans and
a sweatshirt like everyone else.

Slowly I began to meet people. I turned
sixteen and by the winter of 1981 I had black
friends for the first time in my life. Although
I could hardly shout it from the rooftops, I
wanted to. I had started going to parties in
Bethnal Green and Stoke Newington and Mile
End. I was falling in love with a boy from my
A-Level English class. There was only one
problem: I was leading a double life.

Before Mum and Dad had left for Sydney
they had billeted me with a family of Catholic
aristocrats who lived in a very large house in
South Kensington. Their daughter, Eloise, was
my oldest and closest friend, but the life she was
leading did not easily merge with mine. That

year, she was 'coming out', which in her world did not mean declaring her homosexuality, but 'doing the season': in other words, she was a debutante. This meant being photographed for magazines like *Harpers & Queen* and *Tatler*, attending tea parties in other large houses with other young heiresses and going to charity balls. Once I borrowed one of her voluminous, silk ball dresses, with a bodice that felt as though it was cutting off the blood supply to my bosom, and went with her. It was called the White Knight's Ball and it was held in a smart hotel off Park Lane to raise money for the Order of Malta, a 'noble' Catholic order of which Eloise's father and eldest brother were distinguished members. Dressing up was, as usual, the best part of the evening and once I realized that the place was filled with boys who danced like horses trying to kick their shoes off, I sat most of it out, resting my poor breasts on the table and chain-smoking Benson and Hedges. By this stage public schoolboys had lost their charm for me but, loaded up with champagne, I did try kissing one that evening and noticed, as his large teeth ground into mine, that they also kissed like horses.

After that I fell into the arms of Mark, the boy in my English class. My heart goes out to him for his patience because for almost a year (my sisters will shudder to read this) I withheld my virginity, willingly abandoning myself to endless snogging and through-the-trousers kneading. We would spend hours on his mum's bed in Islington, heavy petting to the soundtrack of *Midnight Express*.

Through Mark I became close friends with a girl called Kelly who lived with her parents on a council estate in Dalston. When Thatcher brought in the Right to Buy policy, Kelly's dad, a retired dustman, gloomily predicted the demise of his class: 'That's how she'll have us in the end. She'll buy us off.' With Kelly's help I began, along with the rest of the students in my year, to despise Margaret Thatcher. She and Denis had lived round the corner from us when we were growing up and I had retrospective fantasies about shooting her in the chest on Chelsea Manor Street and changing the course of British history. Kelly took me on protest marches, for the 'right to work', for nuclear disarmament, for sanctions against South Africa, against spending cuts and the 'sus law' and Cruise missiles on British soil. I remember the particular fatigue that came with the sustained slowness of marching, the insidious cold, and the joy when it was over and I could wrap my hands around a mug of tea and sit listening to everyone arguing about the attendance figures. I remember, on one of those marches, Kelly and I gleefully shouting into each other's faces, 'When the Tories get up your nose . . . Picket!' I also remember my hatred of Thatcher intensifying one May morning as I was dressing for college in my charming, sunlit attic bedroom in that large house in Kensington and the news came over the radio of Bobby Sands' death from hunger strike. I had no idea, of course, that my political rage was mostly a smokescreen for profound unease.

For that daily journey between Gloucester Road and King's Cross had become a kind of airlock between two worlds. Soon I began making the journey at night. I would put on a coat over my nightdress and sneak out of my room on the top floor of that large house, slip down the wide, carpeted stairs to the hall, where a carriage clock ticked grandly, unlock the door and ride the Tube to King's Cross and then to Angel. There I would walk along the canal to Mark's house where I would stay until dawn, unmolested by his mother (a prominent feminist whose only concern was whether or not I was using birth control). I would then catch the first Tube back to Kensington and slip back to my bed unnoticed by my host family, or so I thought at the time. As it turned out, Eloise's mother had put a call in to Australia. She didn't mention my midnight flits across London, but she did ask my mother if she was aware that I was sleeping with a black boy. When I told Mum that Mark's father was Kenyan, she went dewy-eyed and asked where, exactly, he was from.

I remember sitting in 'the library' one evening, watching the news with Eloise's father, a peer in the House of Lords. The room was painted Chinese yellow and there was a chandelier that, at certain times of the day, cast drops of rainbow light on to the walls. On the television, Brixton was in flames. We sat there in silence watching the footage of the day's riots. When the news was over I dared to look over at him, trying to frame some conciliatory, non-committal sentence that might not be too great a betrayal of my own feelings, but he stood up, walked over to the set, switched it off and walked out of the room.

Meanwhile Dad had started to put pressure on me to join them in Australia. He sent me a prospectus for Sydney University and suggested that I apply. I didn't want to leave London. I was a teenager in full self-dramatization mode and believed that my life must be in England: I would be a writer and, with time, I would take on the Tory regime. But Dad dug in his heels. I would have to think of a better reason not to go to Australia. That was how the idea came of applying to Oxford, the one and only place that I knew Dad would accept as an alternative to Sydney. Even if I didn't get in, I thought, sitting the exam would at least delay the application process for a year, and by then, who knew? Anything could happen.

In the end I didn't go to Australia, but Fly did. By the winter of 1981 she could, as she put it, no longer *handle her habit*, a chilling euphemism for the state her life was in. Work had dried up and she was signing on. One weekend I went to London from Oxford to stay with her in her basement. She lived in her bed, watched TV and ate Hot Oat Cereal. I never saw her shooting up but I remember the bloodstains on her sheets.

I rang Mum and Dad and told them that Fly might die unless we could get her some help. This was not idle dramatizing. Many of her friends from that era would end up dead or in prison. Remembering, no doubt, their own powerlessness in the years before they had left England, on the phone my parents hedged. Maybe later, they suggested. Driven by that teenage theatricality, I slammed down the phone and marched off to see the bank manager to ask him if I could borrow £360 for a ticket to Sydney for my sister who was a heroin addict. I sat in his office and told him that I was worried that if she didn't go she would overdose. I don't know who that man was, or what spirit was animating him that day, but he lent me the money. I bought the ticket and Fly had her last fix in the plane toilets.

That summer I left the house in South Kensington and the college in King's Cross, and so ended my year of living dangerously on the class divide. I went to live with Izzy and her boyfriend in Putney and enrolled in another ILEA college in Hammersmith where a loud minority of delinquent Sloane Rangers set about proving to the majority that this was their decade.

Izzy mothered me through my first heartbreak,

my first moped accident, my exams
and all the usual dramas of teenage life.
Together we watched the Falklands crisis
unfold, and then the miners' strike, both of us
stupefied by the terrifying deftness with which
Thatcher seemed to be lastingly changing
people's minds. We found ourselves, along with
the rest of the country, giving up active protest
in favour of a detached scepticism. At Izzy's
dinners, political debate gave way to risqué
party games, and the drug of choice moved
from pot to cocaine. During that time, Izzy was
looking, as ever, to augment her income. (She
was earning a paltry salary working for a small
publishing firm off Notting Hill Gate called
Virgin Books which was run by a man called
Richard Branson whose list included titles like
Cluck! The True Story of Chickens in the Cinema and
Rockstars in Their Underpants.) She decided to try
her hand as a coke dealer and managed to leave
her handbag (containing some scales and the
newly scored drugs) on the Underground. She
realized her mistake on the walk home from

the station and was white with fear when she stepped through the front door. Her boyfriend would kill her if he found out. What was she going to do? Then the phone rang and a man with a Scottish accent asked, 'Did you leave something on the Tube?'

Had he opened her bag? Of course he had. In fact he had touched the scales and was terrified he had left his 'dabs' on them, thinking that it was heroin and fearing that it would be pinned on him if he was caught with it. He was torn between his fear and his curiosity, a curiosity well rewarded by the posh girl who answered his call.

'I've never done this before,' Izzy said. 'I'll never do it again . . .'

Izzy wanted desperately for him to give back the coke, as she stood to make about £300 on it (which, in 1982, was a considerable sum), but she sensed there was little hope of that. His voice had a menacing calm about it. He asked her to meet him outside Notting Hill Gate Tube station. They went to his room in a cheap hotel round the corner to collect the bag. Then they went downstairs and he made Izzy scatter the coke in the gutter. Izzy thought about running away with it, but she did what he asked. It was a sobering experience for her to see herself through his eyes. He, an oil rigger from Glasgow, just couldn't understand why a young woman from a privileged background had become involved in drugs.

Soon after that Izzy met her French husband and I met mine and we both ran away to join Beatrice in Paris where, so it seemed, people still believed in politics and mass demonstration and the idea of equality and were doggedly refusing to accept the new global consensus. Thanks, in part, to Gran and her intricate snobberies, all of us would ultimately feel excluded from that consensus. Like me, Izzy and Beatrice chose to stay in a society relatively untouched by the all-out consumerism that would blossom in Britain from the eighties onwards. Cissy would join the New Age revival and flee to southern Spain to start a yoga retreat, moving back ten years later to settle in the West Country where she is now

pursuing her dream of being a singer. Fly has
been clean for over twenty years and is still – in
spite of herself and much to her chagrin that
I should even mention it – very much a Head.
As for me, the prejudices I inherited from my
Edwardian grandmother were not likely to
be challenged by the elitist education I would
receive at Oxford, and so I ended up living,
as she did, in the middle of nowhere. In the
Cevennes, one of France's wildest and remotest
corners, I'm removed from everything Gran
despised. I realize, too, that I'm at the age
Dad was when he lost his business and Eileen
was when she met her final lover, Kole. In the
mythology of my family it is an age when new
lives and new creeds begin.

As I was coming to the end of writing this,
Dad died in Sydney after a short and spirited
battle with cancer. To the last, he had bottles
of claret smuggled into the hospice by friends
and he won the nurses over by singing snatches
of Cole Porter to them and kissing their hands.
The young Australian wife he spent the last

twenty years of his life with agreed that he would have wanted a Chelsea send-off, so we organized a memorial service for him in the church where we had sometimes occupied a pew, shamelessly belting out the descant.

All five sisters and brother Joe were there in the front row with Dad's brave, beautiful widow, and Mum, a little further back, looking slightly stricken by what her children might do next. Laurent was there, next to my new in-laws, and all twelve grandchildren. Uncle Henry had died at the beginning of the year, but his big laughter poured forth from his daughter, warming or shocking the congregation, which seemed to be a perfect blend of Heads and Straights.

We all sang Dad's two favourite hymns and then Cissy sang Nat King Cole's 'Smile', Fly offered snatches of Peter Cook, the organist was prevailed upon to play 'The Girl From Ipanema', the incumbent vicar wept for the first time in his career and we all walked out of the church behind a piper singing, 'I'll take the high road and you'll take the low road' in broad Scottish accents. In the pub afterwards, where the long afternoon's emotion was washed down by reassuring quantities of alcohol, we sang 'Frank Mills' from *Hair*, and on the bench outside the pub, Izzy and Cissy could be found sharing a joint with two of the old Westminster gang. As one of them put it to me in an email the following day, 'There's hope for the future.'

In my own tribute, I shared with the congregation a memory that I felt captured my father's spirit. It is 1972 and I am eight. Dad is holding me firmly by the wrists and dangling me from the top of the Pont du Gard, a Roman aqueduct in France about 160 feet high. We're grinning gleefully at each other and I feel both utterly endangered and utterly safe, the particular combination which, I realize, we have all been looking for in our lives ever since.

Acknowledgements

This book would not have been possible without
the help of my family. I would like to thank my
mother for her courage in answering my questions;
my eldest sister, Louise (Bee), for having pushed me,
despite all my misgivings, to tackle this subject in the
first place; my sister Catherine (Izzy) for her support
and her candour; my sister Amynta (Fly) for her
strength and her remarkable ability to tell it as it is;
Cissy, whose life merits a book of its own, and my
dear brother, Tom (Joe), whose benign, unwavering
presence sustains us all.

I am also grateful to my late uncle, Charles
Fox (Henry), a hellraiser who not only filled our

lives with fun, but who was also a gifted writer who taught me the trade. I have him to thank for encouraging his mother, Enid Duncan (Eileen), to sit down as an old lady and put her life on tape. Those delightful tapes provided much of my material and it is, as I came to realize as I was writing this little book, her indomitable spirit overarching the whole. I'm grateful to all the other members of this weird and wonderful family – some of whom I've mentioned – be they Heads or Straights.

My thanks also go to Helen Conford at Penguin Press for seeking me out and for trusting me, to Anthony Goff for his faith, to the London Underground for giving me the opportunity to dig down and take a good look at where I come from and to Luthfa Begum for helping me to bite the bullet. (In the run-up to publishing this book I received a message from one of the reps at Penguin. She knew Luthfa. Would I like her email address? With some trepidation, I wrote to Luthfa, sending her what I had written. 'Funny thing,' she wrote back. 'I went to Kingsway too – ten years later – and loved it. Like you, it was the first time I properly met and got to know people from outside my Bengali community and my bit of the East End and it led to my own double existence for a few years. Amazing, the similarities, and I'd like to think it's why we clicked that evening. It was brilliant fun and I do remember pushing the tables back and having a dance.')

PENGUIN LINES
Choose Your Journey

If you're looking for...

Romantic Encounters

Heads and Straights
by Lucy Wadham
(the Circle line)

Waterloo–City, City–Waterloo
by Leanne Shapton
(the Waterloo & City line)

Tales of Growing Up and Moving On

Heads and Straights
by Lucy Wadham
(the Circle line)

A Good Parcel of English Soil
by Richard Mabey
(the Metropolitan line)

Mind the Child
by Camila Batmanghelidjh and Kids Company
(the Victoria line)

The 32 Stops
by Danny Dorling
(the Central line)

*A History of Capitalism
According to the Jubilee Line*
by John O'Farrell
(the Jubilee line)

A Northern Line Minute
by William Leith
(the Northern line)

Mind the Child
by Camila Batmanghelidjh and
Kids Company
(the Victoria line)

Heads and Straights
by Lucy Wadham
(the Circle line)

Laughter and Tears

Breaking Boundaries

Drift
by Philippe Parreno
(the Hammersmith & City line)

Buttoned-Up
by Fantastic Man
(the East London line)

Waterloo–City, City–Waterloo
by Leanne Shapton
(the Waterloo & City line)

Earthbound
by Paul Morley
(the Bakerloo line)

Mind the Child
by Camila Batmanghelidjh
and Kids Company
(the Victoria line)

The Blue Riband
by Peter York
(the Piccadilly line)

**A Bit of
Politics**

The 32 Stops
by Danny Dorling
(the Central line)

*A History of Capitalism
According to the Jubilee Line*
by John O'Farrell
(the Jubilee line)

**Musical
Direction**

Heads and Straights
by Lucy Wadham
(the Circle line)

Earthbound
by Paul Morley
(the Bakerloo line)

The Blue Riband
by Peter York
(the Piccadilly line)

*What We Talk About When
We Talk About The Tube*
by John Lanchester
(the District line)

*A Good Parcel of
English Soil*
by Richard Mabey
(the Metropolitan line)

**Tube
Knowledge**

**A Breath of
Fresh Air**

*A Good Parcel of
English Soil*
by Richard Mabey
(the Metropolitan line)

**Design for
Life**

Waterloo–City, City–Waterloo
by Leanne Shapton
(the Waterloo & City line)

Buttoned-Up
by Fantastic Man
(the East London line)

Drift
by Philippe Parreno
(the Hammersmith & City line)